WORLD'S
GREATEST
ATHLETES

Tim DUNCAN

By John Walters

The
Child's
World®

www.childsworld.com

Published in the United States of America by The Child's World®
P.O. Box 326 • Chanhassen, MN 55317-0326
800-599-READ • www.childsworld.com

ACKNOWLEDGMENTS

The Child's World®: Mary Berendes, Publishing Director

Produced by Shoreline Publishing Group LLC
President / Editorial Director: James Buckley, Jr.
Designer: Tom Carling, carlingdesign.com
Assistant Editor: Ellen Labrecque

Photo Credits:
Cover: AP/Wide World
Interior: Corbis: 25. All other images courtesy of AP/Wide World.

LIBRARY OF CONGRESS
CATALOGING-IN-PUBLICATION DATA

Walters, John (John Andrew)
 Tim Duncan / by John Walters.
     p. cm. — (The world's greatest athletes)
 Includes bibliographical references and index.
 ISBN 1-59296-759-0 (library bound : alk. paper)
 1. Duncan, Tim, 1976——Juvenile literature. 2. Basketball players—
United States—Biography—Juvenile literature. I. Title. II. Series.
 GV884.D86W35 2006
 796.323092—dc22

                              2006006285

CONTENTS

Not So Famous, But Fabulous

BEFORE CHRISTMAS OF 2004, THE NATIONAL Basketball Association (NBA) released a list of its 25 best-selling player jerseys. Tim Duncan's No. 21 San Antonio Spurs jersey was only the ninth-most popular on the list.

Clearly other NBA players are more popular than the seven-foot tall center. Among the players whose jerseys sold more were Shaquille O'Neal of the Miami Heat, LeBron James of the Cleveland Cavaliers, and Allen Iverson of the Philadelphia 76ers. These superstars may be the fan favorites, but none them are better players than Tim.

Since joining the league in 1998, Tim has ruled the NBA. He was named the 1998 Rookie of the Year and was named the league's Most Valuable Player (MVP) in 2002 and 2003. He has been voted to play in the All-Star Game nine times. Tim's most **impressive** accomplishment, however, is leading the Spurs to three NBA championships (1999, 2003, 2005).

Tim Duncan may just be the best basketball player in the world. The amazing thing is that he was introduced to the sport by accident. If it were not for a terrible hurricane and a family tragedy, he might never have picked up a basketball.

CHAPTER 1

A Superstar by Accident

TIM DUNCAN WAS BORN ON APRIL 25, 1976, ON THE island of St. Croix in the Virgin Islands.

The Virgin Islands are a tropical paradise located in the Caribbean Sea. They are United States territories. The largest of the Virgin Islands is St. Croix (pronounced "Croy"), located nearly 1,000 miles southeast of Miami, Florida. St. Croix is 28 miles long and seven miles wide, and attracts many tourists with its sunshine and beautiful beaches.

Tim is the youngest of three children. His father, William, was a mason (a bricklayer) and his mother, Ione, was a midwife. Tim has two older sisters named Cheryl and Tricia.

As a boy, swimming—not basketball—was Tim's favorite sport. He and Tricia were two of the best

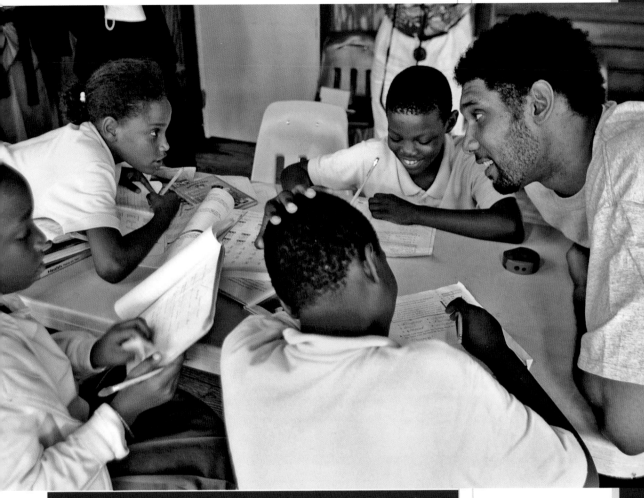

Tim grew up in the Virgin Islands and often returns to work with kids there and show them how to succeed.

swimmers in all of the Virgin Islands. Tricia was so fast in the pool that she competed for the Virgin Islands in the 1988 Summer Olympics. She swam the 100-meter and 200-meter backstroke.

Tim was also swift in the pool, setting records in the 50-meter and 100-meter freestyle for swimmers his age in the Virgin Islands. His records have not yet been broken.

Tim's mom was his biggest fan. She volunteered as a timer for all his meets and her cheers could be heard by her son even when he was underwater. "Every meet she was the loudest parent there," Tim told *Sports Illustrated* in 1995. "I could always pick out

Tim's friends and fans from home in the Virgin Islands have followed him to the NBA, where they show their support.

her voice yelling over everybody else."

Ione Duncan had a favorite motto that she would often repeat to her son. It went like this:

> *Good, better, best.*
> *Never let it rest,*
> *Until your good is better*
> *And your better is best.*

On September 17, 1989, Hurricane Hugo struck St. Croix with tremendous force. (Tim, who still has a reputation for being calm and **serene**, slept through the storm.) The island was slammed hard by high winds and drenching rain. The storm ruined the Olympic-sized swimming pool where Tim swam, the only such pool on the island. For a short time Tim and his team trained in the ocean, but his healthy fear of sharks ended the routine quickly.

Seven months after Hurricane Hugo struck, Tim's life was interrupted by something much more terrible. His mother, his biggest fan, died of cancer on April 24, 1990. It was one day before Tim's 14th birthday. He never swam competitively again.

Tim, who was six feet tall when he began high school, started playing basketball. His sister Cheryl had bought him a basketball hoop for Christmas two years earlier. His dad had planted the pole so deep in the ground that it had survived Hurricane Hugo. The entire island of St. Croix had only four basketball courts at the time.

Cheryl's husband, Ricky Lowery, had played college basketball at a small school in Ohio before returning to the island. Lowery began to tutor his teenage brother-in-law in basketball. He drilled Tim in passing, shooting, and dribbling techniques. Tim would dribble the basketball on stones, up stairs, or while carrying Lowery on his back.

Meanwhile, Tim grew. And grew. And grew. By the time he graduated from St. Dunstan's Episcopal High School, Tim was 6-10—and he could shoot a short jumper with either hand.

Tim averaged 25 points, 12 rebounds, and five blocks per game as a high school senior. Almost no college coaches knew about him, though. One person who did was Dave Odom, the head coach at Wake Forest University, a small college in Winston-Salem, North Carolina. One of Dave's former players, Chris King, had traveled to the Virgin Islands as part of an NBA promotional tour. He watched in awe as Tim,

Tim has very good hands for a big player. He credits his early work on ball handling with Lowery for helping make him such as good passer today.

still in high school, held his own against NBA players. Based on King's praise, Tim was offered a scholarship, which he accepted.

Tim's college debut gave no hint of his future

Though still fairly new to basketball, Tim earned a scholarship to basketball power Wake Forest University.

Tim's height and shooting skills made him a force around the hoop.

greatness. He played his first game on the first day he ever saw snow, when Wake Forest visited the University of Alaska-Anchorage. He did not score a point or even attempt a shot.

That was the last quiet game that Tim, a quiet person, ever played for Wake Forest. Playing in the Atlantic Coast Conference (ACC), the toughest basketball conference in the country, Tim led the Demon Deacons, to a pair of ACC championships. He was an excellent scorer, averaging 20 points per game during his final two years of school. He was an even better defensive player, though.

Tim was named the national Defensive Player of the Year three straight seasons at Wake Forest. With his long arms he was able to block more shots than all but one player in the history of college basketball (that player, Adonal Foyle of Colgate University, is also a native of the Caribbean).

With his quick reflexes and long arms, Tim played defense as if he were Doc Ock, that famous enemy of Spider-man. "It seems like every time you turn around he's staring you in the face," said one opposing player after watching Tim score 18 points, grab 20 rebounds, and block three shots in a Wake Forest win. "I could have sworn there were four or five Tim Duncans out there."

As a senior Tim won the Naismith Award and the Wooden Award. Those awards are given every year to the most outstanding college basketball player in the country. As amazing as Tim's basketball skills were, opposing coaches and players and even fans began to notice something else about Tim: his attitude. Tim was not only mature, he was **unflappable**. Nothing that happened on the court, good or bad, could alter the blank expression on his face.

"Emotion doesn't work for me," Tim told *Sports Illustrated*. "If your opponent picks up on your frustration, then you're at a disadvantage."

As Tim neared the end of his senior year of

college, it was clear to everyone that there was something special about this giant. "Some day your six-year-old kid will ask you for a Tim Duncan jersey for Christmas," one opposing coach told his players before they took the court against Wake Forest. "This is your chance to play a future NBA Hall of Famer,

Tim was the college player of the year for 1997. He shared the stage with coach of the year Clem Haskins of Minnesota.

Young Tim Duncan

- Favorite book as a young boy was Encyclopedia Brown, a series of stories about a boy detective

- Didn't start playing organized basketball until the ninth grade—once he started, he couldn't put the ball down!

- Started wearing his shorts backwards at practice as a freshman at Wake Forest—and he still does so today!

your turn to face the greatest player any of you will ever meet."

That June, two wonderful things occurred in Tim Duncan's life. First, he graduated from Wake Forest with a degree in **psychology** (the study of the human mind). Second, he was made the first overall pick in the 1997 NBA draft by the San Antonio Spurs. The island kid was going pro!

Tim teamed with David Robinson (50) to give the Spurs a pair of powerful and talented big men.

CHAPTER 2

A Champion in Many Ways

DURING THE FIRST MONTH OF TIM DUNCAN'S NBA career in 1997, the Spurs played the Houston Rockets in a preseason game. One of the Rockets that night was Charles Barkley, a 6-6 forward who four seasons earlier had been named the league's MVP. After playing against Tim that evening, Charles told the **media**, "I have seen the future and he wears number 21. Tim's even better than I thought he was, and I was expecting good stuff."

Because Tim was the first overall pick in the draft, a lot of people placed high **expectations** on him. The Spurs had finished the previous season with an awful 20–62 record, but that mark was misleading. Their best player, seven-foot center David Robinson, had missed almost the entire season because of an injury. Now Robinson was back. With he and Tim in the same starting lineup, the NBA's worst team instantly changed into one of its best.

Tim played power forward, where some of the league's toughest players would match up against him. Muscle-bound players such as Karl Malone Dennis Rodman, and Charles Oakley would test his toughness every game. "I think everyone wants to see what you'll take and what you won't take," Tim said. "You have to accept that and never back down."

Tim never did. In his first game against the Chicago Bulls and Rodman, one of the best rebounders of all time, Tim grabbed 22 **boards**. It was that kind of season. Tim was the only rookie named to play in the 1998 All-Star Game. He averaged 21 points and 12 rebounds per game and was easily selected as the NBA Rookie of the Year.

The Spurs went from 20–62 in 1996-97 to 56–26 in 1997-98. Though they lost in the second round of the playoffs to the Utah Jazz, they had made the second-biggest one-year improvement in NBA history.

Fame and pro success did not change Tim. He kept dating his college sweetheart, Amy Sherrill, whom he married in 2001. He persuaded his best friend at Wake Forest, Mark Scott, to move to San Antonio with him and become his business manager. His quirky habits, such as collecting knives and samurai swords ("I like sharp things," Tim explained) or wearing his gym shorts backward, did not cease. Tim also likes to cut the sleeves off his T-shirts and joked that he might come up with a line of clothing called "Ultimate Rejects" wear.

Tim was the NBA's rookie of the year after helping the Spurs make a big turnaround in the 1997-98 season.

The Spurs beat the New York Knicks in five games in the NBA Finals to win their first NBA championship in 1999.

In Tim's second season, the NBA experienced a **lockout**. Players and owners could not agree on important business issues and so the season did not start on time. The lockout was a tense time for

NBA players and fans, but Tim did not let it bother him. "When people asked me about when I thought the lockout would end, I'd whisper, 'February 10, but don't tell anybody,'" Tim said. "I just do goofy stuff like that to get a reaction. Life is too short to be serious all the time."

When the lockout did end, the NBA played a shortened 50-game season. Tim and David Robinson led the Spurs to a 37–13 record, which tied for the league's best. Tim started every game and his averages in points (21.7) and rebounds (11.4) were as strong as his rookie season.

In the Western Conference playoffs, Tim took his stellar play to a new level. In the first round the Spurs beat the Minnesota Timberwolves, led by seven-foot star Kevin Garnett, four games to one.

In the next round, the Spurs met the Los Angeles Lakers, who had two of the biggest stars in the NBA—Shaquille O'Neal and Kobe Bryant—on their side. Tim was outstanding, averaging 29 points per game as the Spurs swept the Lakers 4–0. The Spurs also swept their next opponent, the Portland Trail Blazers, to qualify for the NBA Finals for the first time in franchise history. In the Finals, the Spurs played the

Why a lockout? Team owners and players could not agree on how to divide the money that teams earn from fans and TV contracts. Once they agreed, the lockout ended.

Eastern Conference champion New York Knicks.

If Tim was excited about playing for an NBA championship, he never let it show. Writers hailed him as the "Quiet Giant." The second-year pro continued to show the **poise** uncommon in someone just 23 years old. One writer asked him if he was considered the best. "Some people do, some people

One of Tim's biggest strengths is, well, his strength! He uses inside moves like this one to get closer to the basket.

don't," answered Tim. "It doesn't really matter."

Tim was the best in the Finals. He averaged 27 points and 14 rebounds per game. The Spurs beat the Knicks, four games to one, to win their first NBA championship. Tim was an NBA champion less than ten years after he'd stopped swimming.

Suddenly, the NBA could not stop talking about the San Antonio power forward who rarely spoke. Tim Duncan was the Spur of the moment.

CHAPTER 3

The Best Keeps Getting Better

SAN ANTONIO CONTINUED THEIR WINNING WAYS in the 1999–2000 season. The Spurs raced out to a 14–3 record and Tim, averaging career highs in points (23.7) and rebounds (12.4), looked ready to lead San Antonio back to the NBA Finals. He was named co-MVP (along with Shaquille O'Neal) of the NBA All-Star Game. His West squad won 137–126 and he scored 24 points and had 14 rebounds.

Late in the season, however, Tim suffered a bad knee injury. He missed the rest of the season and the Spurs were eliminated from the playoffs early.

Once Tim's knee was healthy again, he continued to improve while the Spurs continued to dominate. He has been named an All-NBA first team player in each of his first eight seasons in the league. Only four other players in NBA history have ever done that. He has also been named to the first or second All-NBA defensive team in each of first eight seasons as well.

But Tim has never cared about personal glory. "He's unbelievably humble," says former Spurs teammate Steve Kerr. "He cares nothing about personal stats. He blames himself when we lose."

Fortunately, Tim does not lose often. Before the

Tim has been an All-Star in every year of his career. He is shown here in white during the 2005 All-Star Game.

Tim's Big Moment

The NBA Finals marked a big turning point in Tim Duncan's life and in the life of the San Antonio Spurs. The series against the New Jersey Nets would be the last for longtime Spurs star David "The Admiral" Robinson. The dominating center earned his nautical

nickname during his college years at the U.S. Naval Academy; he actually put off his NBA career for more than a year to complete his military service.

Though David had made the Spurs very good, it was not until Tim Duncan came along that the team became great. The 2003 Finals would be the last time the two would play together, and the game represented a real passing of the torch.

As it turned out, "torched" is what Finals MVP Duncan did to the Nets, especially in the last game of San Antonio's four-game sweep.

Afterward, however, Tim thought not of stats, but of his friend. "In the last couple of seconds of the game, I was thinking, I'm not going to play with this guy again. It's going to be weird."

2005-2006 season began, Tim had missed a total of 38 games. In those games the Spurs' record was 20–18 (.526). In the games that Tim played, the Spurs were 418–168 (.713).

In 2002, Tim was voted the league's Most Valuable Player after averaging 25.5 points and 12.7 rebounds per game. He scored a career-high 53 points on December 26 in a game against the Dallas Mavericks. The Spurs, for the second straight season, led the NBA in attendance. But, also for the second straight season, San Antonio was knocked out of the playoffs by the Los Angeles Lakers.

The following season was David Robinson's last. Tim wanted to send his teammate and friend out in style—and he did. The Spurs dominated the NBA with a 60–22 record. Tim was named NBA MVP again and this time led the Spurs back to the NBA Finals.

There they faced the New Jersey Nets. For the second time Tim was named the Finals MVP. He averaged 24 points, 17 rebounds and five blocks as the Spurs won four games to two. In the deciding game, Tim scored 21 points and had 20 rebounds, 10 assists, and eight blocks.

In 2005, the Spurs made it back to the NBA Finals.

Tim's excellent play had become routine. Again he was named the NBA Finals MVP (for the third time) as the Spurs needed all seven games to beat the previous season's champs, the Detroit Pistons.

In Game 7, which the Spurs won at home, 81–74,

Another Finals, another MVP: Tim hoisted the trophy again in 2005.

he scored 25 points and had 11 rebounds. San Antonio had won three NBA championships in Tim's first eight seasons.

While Tim's Ultimate Rejects wear clothing line has never gotten off the ground, he and his wife, Amy, have created The Tim Duncan Foundation. It is a charity organization that helps fund education, health awareness, and youth sports programs.

Tim remains a private person. Even though he has won more NBA MVP awards than any current player, he does not have an athletic shoe sponsorship. His NBA jersey still isn't a top seller. But Tim doesn't care about any of that. He's just happy to keep winning NBA championships.

Tim Duncan's Career Statistics

SAN ANTONIO

Season	G	Pts.	PPG.	RPG	APG	BPG
1997-98	82	1,731	21.1	11.9	2.7	2.51
1999	50	1,084	21.7	11.4	2.4	2.52
1999-2000	74	1,716	23.2	12.4	3.2	2.23
2000-01	82	1,820	22.2	12.2	3.0	2.34
2001-02	82	2,089	25.5	12.7	3.7	2.48
2002-03	81	1,884	23.3	12.9	3.9	2.93
2003-04	69	1,538	22.3	12.4	3.1	2.68
2004-05	66	1,342	20.3	11.1	2.7	2.64
2005-06	80	1,485	18.6	11.0	3.2	2.03
Career	666	14,689	22.1	12.0	3.1	2.40

LEGEND: G: Games; **Pts.**: Points; **PPG**: Average points per game; **RPG**: average rebounds per game; **APG**: Assists per game; **BPG**: Blocks per game

GLOSSARY

boards   nickname for rebounds

expectations   thoughts or predictions that people have for the future

impressive   well-received, awe-inspiring

lockout   when a pro sports league prevents its players from playing due to a contract dispute

media   general term for newspapers, radio, TV, and the Internet

poise   great coolness under pressure

psychology   study of the human mind and how it thinks

serene   peaceful

unflappable   not easily excited

BOOKS

Tim Duncan (Basketball's New Wave)
> By Mark Stewart
> (Millbrook Press, Connecticut) 2000
> This book covers Duncan's rise as one of the NBA's elite
> players after he led his team to the franchise's first-ever
> NBA championship.

Tim Duncan: Greatest Stars Of The NBA 2004
> By Jon Finkel
> (TokyoPop, Los Angeles) 2004
> This book celebrates Duncan's leadership skills after he led
> his team to a second NBA title.

Tim Duncan: NBA Reader
> By Scott Howard Cooper
> (Scholastic, New York) 2005
> This book follows Duncan's career from high school, through
> college, to the San Antonio Spurs.

Tim Duncan: Sports Great
> By John Albert Torres
> (Enslow Publishers, New Jersey) 2002
> This book highlights the early stages of Duncan's great
> career.

Tim Duncan (Sports Heroes and Legends)
> By Sean Adams
> (Lerner Publishing Group, Minneapolis) 2004
> This book reviews Duncan's accomplishments and places
> his career in historical context.

WEB SITES

Visit our home page for lots of links about Tim Duncan:
www.childsworld.com/links

Note to Parents, Teachers, and Librarians: We routinely check our Web links to
make sure they're safe, active sites—so encourage your readers to check them out!

INDEX

ABOUT THE AUTHOR

John Walters, a former staff writer for *Sports Illustrated*, is the author of several basketball books, including *Basketball for Dummies* (cowritten with former Notre Dame coach Digger Phelps) and *Same River Twice*, about the University of Connecticut women's team.